Who Can I Love?

THE COOKIE CLUB

Written by Richard H. Slatin, MC/MFCT
Illustrated by Suzy Almblade

Dedication

This book is dedicated to my lovely wife, Aurora, for her ongoing support, with special thanks to Mary, family members, clients, colleagues, and many others for their contributions. Finally, to all the children, who deserve to enjoy their childhood. Please remember this: **"It's All About The Kids!"**

Who Can I Love?

A Cookie Club Book

© 2008 by: Richard H. Slatin, MC/MFCT

All rights reserved.

No part of this book may be reproduced or transmitted in any form, by any means, electronic or mechanical, including photocopying, recording, or by any information storage and retrieval system without written permission from the author or publisher.

DCCS Publishing

400 W. Camelback Rd. Ste. 112

Phoenix, Arizona 85013

www.divorceme.com

SECOND PRINTING

October, 2010

ISBN: **978-0-615-24441-9**

Introduction

This book is intended to be used a resource to help parents and child(ren) understand that it's healthy and okay to love new family members. In today's families, the parents may or may not be married to each other. Regardless of marital status, a family is created when children are born.

As the family structure changes, new people may join the family, such as a parent's significant other or spouse. While it's natural for children to experience love and attachment to this person, often they look to their parents for approval. If the natural parent feels that their role, love, and bond with the child is displaced by the new member, feelings of jealousy, anger, or bitterness, for example, may be expressed. However, when a parent's disapproval is expressed, a child can feel conflicted, even depressed. This can lead to any number of negative behaviors and/or impairment of a child's healthy development.

The message for the parents is: **"It's All About The Kids!"**

Kayden and his parents

Charlie loved cookies. He loved his room, he loved his home, he even loved his turtle. But most of all, Charlie loved making cookies. Charlie's best friends were Angelica, José, and Kayden, and they loved making cookies, too. When they played together, it was like a Club. They had their very own Club, so they called it "The Cookie Club." They loved their Club, because they always had cookies when they were together. So, they were together a lot.

They all went to school together, and after school they played at each other's homes on Mondays, Tuesdays, and Wednesdays. Every week they spent time at each other's home. On some days, they were at Charlie's home. On other days, they were at Kayden's home. On even more other days, they would play at José and Angelica's home. At every home they played in, they had their Club, and they always got cookies with juice or milk after they played. My, how they loved their Cookie Club!

One day, they were playing at Kayden's home, and Kayden was feeling very sad. Kayden's Mom gave them cookies and juice, but after they had their cookies, Kayden was still sad. Charlie, José, and Angelica all wondered why Kayden was sad.

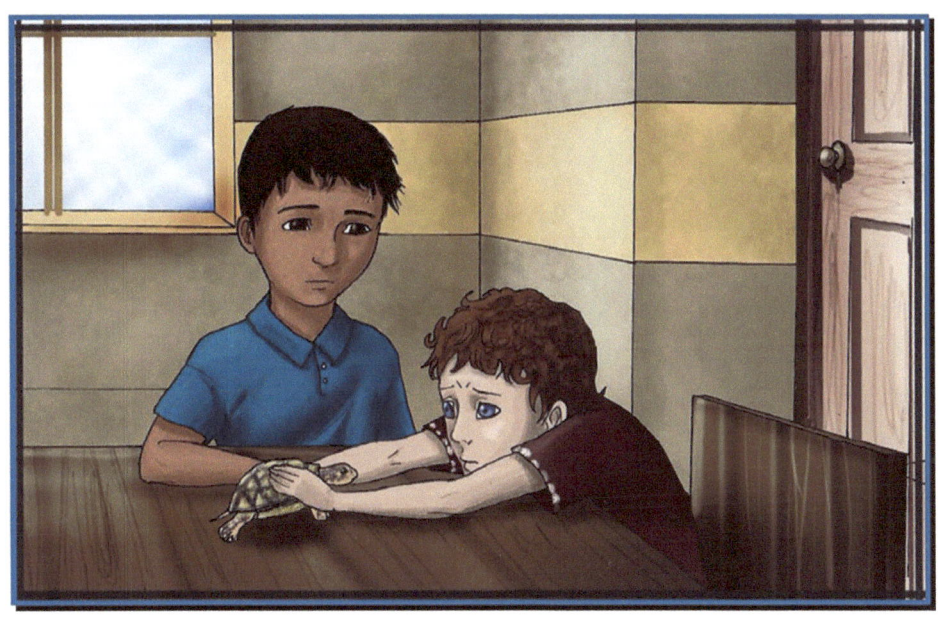

Until two years ago, Kayden's Mom and Dad and Kayden used to live together, but one day they began arguing. Sometimes they were very loud, and sometimes they were very, very quiet. This made Kayden feel sad, and sometimes his stomach hurt.

His Mom and Dad told Kayden that they both loved him, but that it would be better for all of them if they didn't all live together anymore. Then Kayden's Dad moved to another home, but not very far away. Now, sometimes Kayden lives with his Mom and sometimes Kayden lives with his Dad.

But that wasn't why Kayden was sad. Not long ago, Kayden's Dad married a very nice woman named Suzi. When he stayed overnight with his Dad, Suzi sometimes read a bedtime story to him.

She also sang songs to him, and told him funny stories that made him laugh. But best of all, when Kayden's friends came over to play, she made cookies for all of them.

When he was with his Dad and Suzi, he was happy and laughed a lot. When Kayden was with his Mom, he was happy and laughed a lot, too. He loved being with all of them. But, sometimes after he came back from his Dad's home, his Mom would remind him that Suzi wasn't his Mom, and also that maybe Kayden should not like her too much. Kayden knew Suzi was not his Mom, but he <u>liked</u> liking her. Kayden didn't know why he shouldn't like Suzi, but he wanted to mind his Mom. Thinking about this made Kayden feel very sad and confused, and sometimes made his stomach hurt.

    The next day they were all playing at José's and Angelica's house, and Kayden was feeling sad again. Charlie asked Kayden, "Why do you look so sad?" "My Mom says that I shouldn't like Suzi," replied Kayden, "but, I really like her." Now, they had all played at Kayden's Dad's home, and knew Suzi. They all liked Suzi because she made them laugh and read stories to them and she also made them cookies, just like their Moms. They really liked the cookies Suzi made for them!

José and Angelica lived with their Mother, Father, and Grandparents. At dinner, they talked about Kayden.

"Abuelito," José asked his Grandfather, "why wouldn't Kayden's Mom want him to like Suzi?"

"Well," said Abuelito, "your Mother has met Suzi, and says that she's very nice." "Yes, both Suzi and Kayden's Mom are very nice," replied Mother, "but maybe Kayden's Mom thinks that if Kayden likes Suzi, then Kayden may not love his Mom anymore, or as much. Maybe that's why she doesn't want Kayden to like her." "But, Mother," said Angelica, "Kayden always loves his Mom, very much."

José thought about this, and asked "is it okay if we like her?" Mother and the Grandparents looked at each other and smiled. Mother replied, "Yes, it's okay if you like her." José and Angelica both smiled, because they liked Suzi, and she made really good cookies for them.

When it was time for bed, their Mother read them a very nice story with a happy ending, as she did most nights.

After Mother finished reading the story, Angelica told José, "Maybe there's a way Kayden can have a happy ending with his Mom about Suzi." "Yes," said José, "let's talk with Charlie about this tomorrow. Maybe we can all help Kayden."

Before school started the next day, José, Angelica, and Charlie all talked about Kayden, and how they could help him.

In class, Charlie sat right next to Kayden in class, and he thought that Kayden looked very sleepy.

When it was time for recess, Charlie talked with Kayden. "Kayden," said Charlie, "you look very sleepy. Did you stay up late last night watching TV?"

"No," replied Kayden, "but, when my Dad took me back to my Mom's after dinner, they said that they wanted to talk, and asked me to go to my room. After awhile, their voices got loud and angry, and then my stomach hurt. I tried to go to sleep, but just couldn't. I just felt really bad."

Right then the bell rang, and it was time to go back to class. As they walked to class, Charlie told Kayden, "Maybe we can all help make that better." Later that day in school, Charlie noticed that Kayden could barely stay awake and do his schoolwork.

After school, Angelica and José played at Charlie's home, but Kayden wasn't there. José called Kayden's Mom, and found out that Kayden was so tired after school that he was taking a nap.

"A nap!" said Charlie.

Angelica said, "We never take naps anymore."

José said, "Naps are for babies, and Kayden's not a baby!"

"Is he sick?" asked Angelica.

"Not really," answered Charlie's Mom, "but he needs help. Maybe there's a way you can help him. Put your thinking caps on, and let's see what you can think of."

After school the next day, they all went back to Charlie's home and saw blank paper and colored pencils on the big table. Kayden liked to draw. In fact, they ALL liked to draw. While they were drawing, Charlie's Mom brought cookies and milk. "Thank you!" they all said, with big, big, smiles. After she left, Angelica told Kayden how lucky he was to get cookies at both his Mom's and Dad's homes. "Yes," thought Kayden, "I <u>am</u> lucky!" José and Angelica looked at each other, and smiled. When Kayden left to get more paper, Angelica told Charlie, "See? Kayden feels better today!" "Yes," said Charlie, "but he still needs our help. What do you think we should draw?"

Just then, Charlie's Mom came back into the room with Kayden, with more drawing paper. "Why don't you draw something about home that makes you feel good," asked Charlie's Mom. José looked at Kayden, and then he asked Charlie's Mom, "since Kayden lives in two homes, shouldn't he draw two pictures?"

"That's a great idea," said Charlie's Mom. "Why don't you draw two pictures, Kayden. Two pictures about things that make you feel good in both your Mom's home and your Dad's home."

When Kayden went home, he showed his Mom what he had drawn. Kayden's drawing was about the time that he and his Mom had gone to the zoo.

"What a happy day that was!" thought Kayden. His Mom laughed as Kayden talked about how his drawing showing how many animals they had seen, and they talked about how much fun they had. Kayden's Mom said that she loved Kayden's drawing very much, and then she put it up in the hallway, on the wall right next to the front door. As she was looking at Kayden's drawing, she thought about how important it was for Kayden to be happy, and wondered what else she could do about that.

At school the next day, Kayden looked happy, and they all had fun playing together at recess. After school, Kayden's Dad picked him up, because this was a day that they went to have dinner with Suzi, play, do schoolwork, and have a good time. Before dinner, Kayden did his schoolwork and Dad and Suzi made dinner.

Kayden then reached into his backpack and took out the drawing he had made about feeling good at his Dad's home.

Kayden had drawn a picture of the time that he, Dad, and Suzi were flying kites at the park.

Looking at the picture, Kayden remembered how much fun they had that day. After dinner, Kayden told his Dad and Suzi that he had a surprise for them. As he said that, Kayden showed them the drawing he had made of their day at the park. "What pretty kites!" exclaimed Suzi. "We sure had fun that day!" laughed Kayden's Dad. Kayden just smiled, and as they all talked about that day, Kayden's smile got bigger and bigger, and Kayden felt very, very, very happy.

After dinner, Kayden did his schoolwork, with a little help from Dad. After Kayden finished, it was time to go to his Mom's home.

When Kayden and his Dad got in the car to drive back to Kayden's Mom's house, they laughed some more.

Buckling up for safety, they also talked about what they would do that weekend, when Kayden would be with his Dad and Suzi.

When they got to Kayden's Mom's home, Kayden's Dad rang the doorbell. When Kayden heard the door opening, he said "Mom, I'm home!"

Kayden still had his big smile and he was happy to be back at his Mom's home, too. As Kayden's Mom opened the door, Kayden ran in and down the hallway, "Goodnight Dad. I love you!" shouted Kayden. "I love you, too, Kayden. Goodnight!" said Kayden's Dad.

Kayden's Mom asked his Dad to stay a moment, inviting him into her home. She said that she had been thinking about something, and wanted to discuss it, if that was okay. "Sure," said Kayden's Dad.

As Kayden's Dad watched Kayden running down the hallway, he noticed the drawing that was on the wall; the one that Kayden had drawn about his time at the zoo with his Mom.

Kayden's Dad smiled and said to Kayden's Mom, "That's a really great drawing; I have one like that, too."

"Really?" asked Kayden's Mom, and then they began to talk about the drawings Kayden had made.

Kayden's Mom and Dad talked about how happy Kayden was when he showed them his drawings. They talked about how good and important it was for Kayden to be happy.

Then they talked about how happy Kayden is when he is at his Dad's home, and how happy Kayden is when he is at his Mom's home. Mostly, they talked about how good and important it is for Kayden to be happy, and that he is very happy when he shows that he loves them, and Suzi, too.

Right then, Kayden's Mom and Dad decided that Kayden being happy was the most important thing in the whole world.

They also decided that Kayden might be very happy if they told him that he could love them both, and love Suzi, too. They decided that this would be very good for Kayden.

They talked about how families can change, but that when changes happen, it's still "all about the kids."

Kayden's Mom and Dad were very happy, too, because together they had found a way to help Kayden to be happy, and to feel very good about himself.

They decided to share this with him, right <u>now</u>, before another minute had passed. "Kayden!" they called, as they walked down the hallway to

Kayden's room. As Kayden came out of his room, he was happy to see them both smiling.

The next day at recess, Charlie kept looking at Kayden. "Something is different about Kayden," Charlie thought. While they were playing, Charlie and Angelica talked about how Kayden was 'different.' All of a sudden they realized <u>what</u> was different about Kayden. Kayden was happy! Kayden was laughing and smiling! In fact, Kayden was happy all day at school, smiling and never once said that his stomach hurt. When they asked him why he was so happy, Kayden just replied, "it's a secret."

All day long they tried to get Kayden to tell them his <u>big, happy, secret</u>, but Kayden would only smile.

When they were playing, Kayden finally told them his Big, Happy, Secret. "My Mom and Dad said that it's okay to love them both and I can even love Suzi, too!" Kayden said with a big smile, "Now I can love <u>all</u> my family!"

Everyone smiled and felt good about Kayden's Big, Happy, Secret.

The End

NOTES

NOTES

www.ingramcontent.com/pod-product-compliance
Lightning Source LLC
Chambersburg PA
CBHW041537040426

42446CB00002B/133